THE
CAIRNGORMS

·THE NATURE OF THE LAND·

COLIN BAXTER · RAWDON GOODIER

First published in Great Britain in 1990 by
Colin Baxter Photography Ltd
Grantown-on-Spey
Moray PH26 3NA
Scotland
and
Scottish Natural Heritage

First published in paperback in 1998

A CIP catalogue record for this book
is available from the British Library.

ISBN 1-900455-72-2

Front cover photograph
Loch an Eilein, Rothiemurchus and the Cairngorm Mountains

Back cover photograph
From Beinn Mheadhoin looking south, Cairngorms

Printed in Great Britain

THE
CAIRNGORMS
·THE NATURE OF THE LAND·

COLIN BAXTER · RAWDON GOODIER

SCOTTISH
NATURAL
HERITAGE

Colin Baxter Photography, Grantown-on-Spey, Scotland

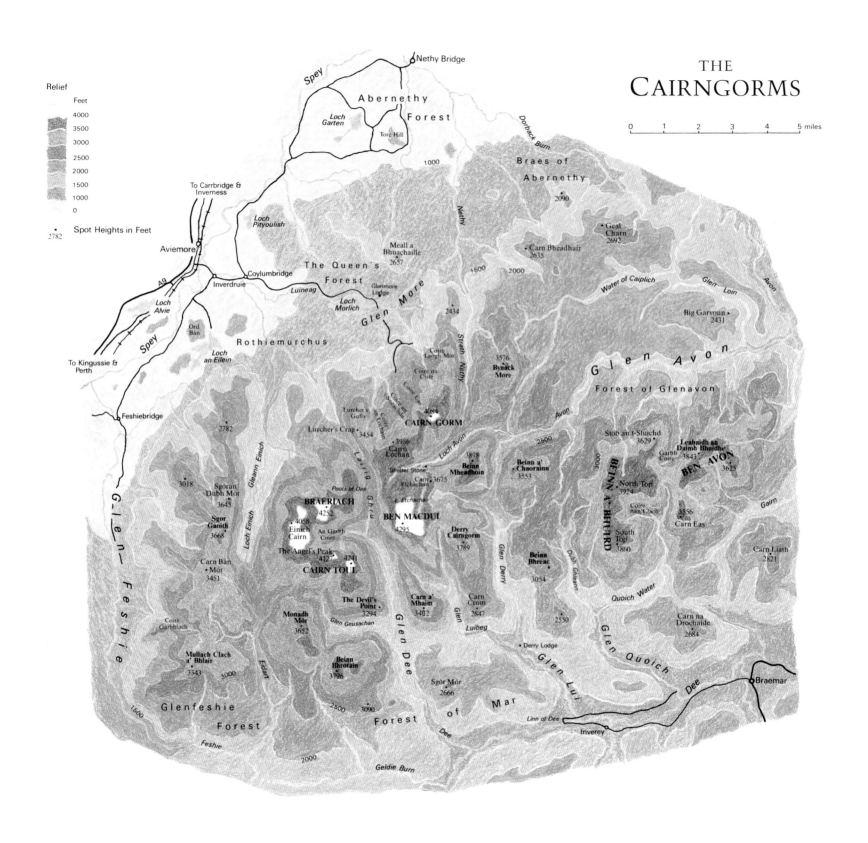

THE
CAIRNGORMS

Relief

Feet
4000
3500
3000
2500
2000
1500
1000
0

2782 · Spot Heights in Feet

0 1 2 3 4 5 miles

Nethy Bridge

Spey

Abernethy

Loch
Garten
Forest

Tore Hill

1000

Dorback Burn

Braes of
Aberethy

2090

To Carrbridge &
Inverness

Loch
Pityoulish

· Geal
Charn
2692

Aviemore

Meall a
Bhuachaille
2657

· Carn Bheadhair
2635

Water of Caiplich

Glen
Loin

Avon

Coylumbridge

The Queen's
Forest

Inverdruie

Luineag

Glenmore
Lodge

Loch
Morlich

1500

2000

Big Garvoun
2431

A9

Glen More

2434

Glen Avon

Loch
Alvie

Ord Bán

Rothiemurchus

Strath Nethy

3576

Bynack
More

Forest of Glenavon

To Kingussie &
Perth

Loch
an Eilein

Coire
Laogh Mór

Coire na
Ciste

Spey

Feshiebridge

Lurcher's
Gully

Lurcher's Crag · 3454

Coire an Lochain

Coire an t-Sneachda

Coire Cas

4084
CAIRN GORM

Stob an t-Sluichd
3629

Leabaidh an
Daimh Bhuidhe
3843

2782 ·

3986
Carn
Lochan

Shelter Stone

Loch Avon

2900

Garbh
Coire

BEN AVON
3625

3018 ·

Sgoran
Dubh Mór
3645

Gleann Einich

3878

Beinn
Mheadhoin

· Beinn a'
Chaorainn
3553

BEINN A' BHUIRD

· North Top
3924

Sgor
Gaoith
3668

Loch Einich

Carn
Etchachan

3675

Coire
nan Clach

3556
Carn Eas

Pools of Dee

Lairig Ghru

· Etchachan

3000

BRAERIACH
4252

Carn Bàn
· Mór
3451

4058
Einich
Cairn

An Garbh
Coire

BEN MACDUI
4295

Derry
Cairngorm
3789

South
Top
3860

Carn Liath
2821

The Angel's Peak
4127 · 4241

CAIRN TOUL

Glen Derry

Beinn
Bhreac
3054

Dubh Ghleann

Quoich Water

Coire
Garbhlach

The Devil's
Point ·
3294

Carn a'
Mhaim
3402

Carn
Crom
2847

Carn na
Drochaide
2684

Monadh
Mór
3652

Glen Geusachan

Glen Dee

Glen
Luibeg

2550

Glen Quoich

Eidart

Mullach Clach
a' Bhlair
3343

3000

Beinn
Bhrotain
3796

· Derry Lodge

Glen Lui

Dee

Braemar

Glenfeshie

Sgòr Mòr
2666

3090

1500

Forest

2500

Forest

of

Mar

Linn of Dee

Inverey

Feshie

2000

Geldie Burn

Scottish Natural Heritage is a government body established
by Parliament in 1992, responsible to the Secretary of State for Scotland.
Its task is to secure the conservation and enhancement of Scotland's unique and
precious natural heritage – the wildlife, the habitats and the landscapes.

SNH aims to help people understand and enjoy Scotland's natural heritage sustainably.

Nowhere is this more important than the Cairngorms. The massif has a
fascinating geological and geomorphological history, and many natural processes are
still active. Here also is the most extensive plateau and upland area in the British Isles, fringed
with some of the finest remnants of our native forests. Both are the home to a diversity
of species including some extremely rare ones. The Cairngorms are inspirational for
the visitor, the onlooker, the ecologist, the hillwalker and many others.

I

For some years I had on my wall a large satellite photograph of Scotland, covering the land from Loch Leven and the Tay in the south to the Cromarty Firth in the north. Seen from a distance its main features were the marked change in the landscape at the highland boundary fault, the great sweep of mountains trending from south-west to north-east known collectively as the Grampians, and the cloud filled glens of the north-west coast. Closer inspection revealed the individual peaks, glens and corries, with their spring snowbeds, and with greater difficulty, patterns of forest, moorlands and high plateau could be distinguished. And in recognising these patterns, one recalled the direct experience of particular mountain places, reflecting on the relations between these indistinct images on the photograph and the infinitely more complex reality of the earth's surface which they represent in summary form.

Photographs taken at ground level are much more familiar to us and we often assume their coincidence with our own vision of the land. Yet they again can surprise us by revealing aspects which we had not registered before. That this should be so is perhaps not surprising given the infinite diversity of the earth's surface, its changes through the seasons and over the course of the years and our own rather intermittent ability to see rather than just look at what is before our eyes. We need to be reminded of the character of this diversity and be able to appreciate directly, rather than merely acknowledge its richness of natural possibilities, because our own actions so often reduce it.

Snowline in Glen Dee. Looking north up the River Dee towards the entrance of the Lairig Ghru, guarded by the Devil's Point.

First impressions of mountains are among memories retained most vividly. Perhaps this stems from the inner anticipatory tension felt when approaching unknown mountain country. Each occasion has its own special flavour generated by both the particular quality of the mountains themselves and the perceiving state of mind. As I cast my mind back, many mountain initiations of particular vividness are recalled – the snow-clad Lakeland hills seen from the train drawing into Coniston station, the first glimpse of Mont Blanc on the way to Chamonix, the vegetated precipices of Mlanje rising out of the African savanna woodland, the amazing snow peaks of the Andes soaring above the arid Peruvian altiplano.

For many of us whose lives have been associated in one way or another with mountains, these initial impressions have imposed themselves upon us as revelations, which the passage of time dims but slowly. For the Cairngorms my first memories are not of hills seen, but rather of an awareness of their snow covered presence when driving up Deeside in the deepening gloom of a winter's evening preceding the great storm between Christmas and New Year 1951/52, walking the last stretch to Bob Scott's bothy at Luibeg, sensing the mountains unseen and waking to the wind's rattle next morning.

This text is a somewhat eccentric account of these wonderful mountains but its eccentricity is not without design. Although their 'natural history' in the deepest sense will be at its heart, I am not attempting a review of this as normally understood – this has already been very well accomplished by others. Rather am I concerned to explore the diverse 'environmental' experience of the Cairngorms through the eyes and ears of those who, like myself, do not have a very deep specialist knowledge of any particular aspect of the hills but who nevertheless seek to be open to the variety of

Cairngorm seen from the northeast over the Braes of Abernethy.

experience which they have to offer, and for whom the experience of the whole appears to be more than the sum of its parts.

My own experience of these hills spans nearly 40 years. I have encountered them as a young climber, a marine snow and mountain warfare instructor, a naturalist studying pinewoods, mountain insects and mountain processes, a conservation bureaucrat and a parent walking with children. Each of these experiences has involved a different perspective, a different way of looking at the hills, which has needed integration. But of course this experience, though diverse, does not encompass all possible perspectives. I am still an outsider – never having lived among them as I have the hills of Wales, nor endeavoured to make a living out of their land, hoed it or hunted it. I respect the rather different perspectives of those who have, but have not presumed to represent them in this rather personal account.

Many writers on the Cairngorms have, with varying success, sought words to epitomise the distinctive character of their subject. Several take pains to emphasise the coherence of the area. Thus John Hill Burton, who published the first book specifically on the Cairngorms in 1864, in his somewhat jocular but often deeply perceptive account of his experiences in the Cairngorms in the first half of the 19th century, observes that:

> When you reach the top [of the Sgor Mor to Sgor Dubh ridge], if the day be clear, the whole Cairngorm range is before you on the other side of the valley, from summit to base . . . from this bird's eye view you at once understand that peculiar structure of the group which makes the valleys so much deeper and narrower, and the precipices so much higher and more abrupt, than those of any other of the Scottish

The Lairig Ghru, the 'Pass of the Dhru burn', one of the two great Cairngorm passes which were used as drove roads for taking cattle to markets in the South.

Mountains. Here there are five summits springing from one root, and all more than four thousand feet above the level of the sea. The circumference of the whole group is as that of one mountain. One might have imagined it to have been a huge wide rounded hill . . . but at some time or other the whole mass had got a jerk in the course of upheavals or subsidences which are so convenient to geologists; and so has been, here and there, split from top to bottom.

Nan Shepherd saw 'the plateau as the true summit of the mountains, they must be seen as a single mountain, and the individual tops, Ben Macdhui, Braeriach and the rest, though sundered from each other by fissures and deep descents, are no more than eddies on the plateau surface.'

W. H. Murray's careful description captures many of the most significant features:

They form plateaux, eroded into granite mountains. At first sight they appear a featureless mass. The flat tops and rounded slopes lack distinctive shape. Our penetration to the interior changes that impression. Their eastern and northern faces are carved into great corries in which dark lochans are ringed by cliffs. The corries spread in ranges along the faces. Nowhere outside Skye can be found so many or such variety within a like area. Outstanding examples are the Garbh Choire between Cairn Toul and Braeriach, whose cliffs form an amphitheatre two miles long and two wide over which spills the infant Dee; the Slochd Mor between Beinn a Bhuird and Ben Avon, the most desolate of all, yet harbouring rare Alpine flora; and that famous corrie between Cairngorm and Ben Macdhui, deep set,

Winter in the Garbh Choire – the 'great rough corrie' of Braeriach 'whose cliffs form an amphitheatre two miles long and two wide over which spills the infant Dee.'

in which lies Loch Avon. It has no match in Scotland, save only at Coruisk, for utter remoteness and the sense of loneliness imparted. The wastes of shattered stone on the summit plateaux form the biggest area of high ground in Britain. Their appeal is not an obvious one. In the act of exploring them, the immense scale on which the scene is set is gradually revealed, and this, with the vast corries, the massive slopes, the long passes, the wide skies, and the very bareness of the ground, where the elements work with a power not known at lower altitudes, gives to these plateaux their distinctive quality – a majesty great enough to cast a spell on man's mind.

II

How is one to approach this mountain region known as the Cairngorms? – both in a real and metaphoric sense – for the manner of approach will influence the impressions we receive and the account we give of our experiences. In his account of the *Natural History of Deeside* written one hundred and fifty years ago, MacGillivray explored the same question saying 'we have to explore this beautiful valley, the glens that open into it, the mountain ranges by which these glens are bounded; and a primary question is, how are we to proceed?' Having as his main focus the Dee, he rapidly came to the conclusion that 'the best way is first to

Cairngorm summit and the northern rim of the central plateau – 'the wastes of shattered stone on the high plateau form the biggest area of high ground in Britain.'

walk along the river to its sources, making digressions, it may be, on occasions, and then, returning, submit to as close an inspection as possible, the various objects to which it may be expedient to direct our attention.' Even though the subject of MacGillivray's concern included just one sector of the Cairngorms, that draining into the Dee, there is much to commend his careful systematic approach of the naturalist. The rivers that flow from a mountain are as much part of the mountain system as the high corries and summits which may be the main goal of the hill walker or mountaineer. Therefore, although we will hopefully reach the summits, we will not hurry too impatiently through the valleys, forests and moorlands which lead us to them. Our appreciation of the character of these higher regions will be influenced by that of our journey towards them.

Three main rivers drain the range, the Spey, the Avon and the Dee, but only the last two can be said to be Cairngorm rivers in the sense of having their source there. The Dee and its tributaries, having the greatest altitudinal range of any river in Britain, can lead us into the heart of the range. Above Braemar, the Dee is essentially an arctic-alpine river and if we follow any of its main tributaries – the Quoich water, the Lui or the Dee itself, its changes as we ascend along its banks will mirror the changes in the surrounding landscape. First, walking through the old lands of long ruined crofts in the lower glens, the water flows past us on beds of unstable shingle (the spawning grounds of the Dee salmon), and over rock slabs and sills. Then, through the steepening heather ground until, climbing their ravines over rock and boulder we are eventually led to the highest lochans in Britain such as Loch Etchachan and Loch Coire an Lochan, devoid of fish and frozen half the year. Most of the water delivered to the lower river by these upper reaches comes from snow melt.

Facing
The River Avon or A'an – thought by some to be so named by the semi legendary third century hero Fionn or Fingal, after his wife Ain who was drowned in its waters at the crossing below Loch A'an. Here pictured near the Bruach, a dozen miles below the ford.

Following pages
Winter sun and swirling cloud in the three north facing corries of Braeriach, the 'brindled heights'.

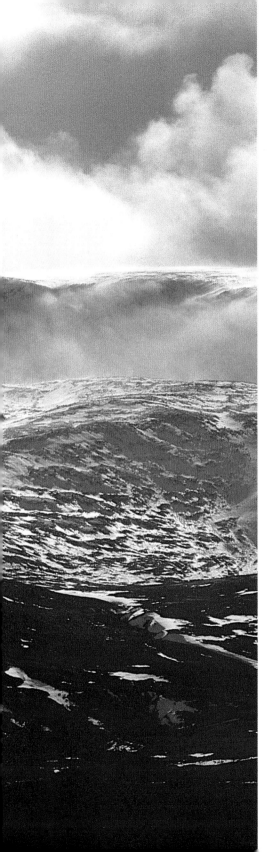

The present-day visitor will generally approach the Cairngorms by one of four routes – the majority via the Drummochter Pass and Upper Speyside, others from the south via Glenshee and Braemar, up Deeside from the direction of Aberdeen or from Inverness and the Slochd Pass in the north. It is only from the last of these directions that the visitor obtains a panoramic view of the range. From all other commonly used approaches the character of the mountains is more elusive, suggested by glimpses and only gradually and partially revealed. Indeed the approach up Deeside is dominated by Lochnagar rather than the Cairngorms, which lie hidden behind their eastern outliers.

Similarly, approaching from Glenshee allows only a very restricted first impression of the massif, a deceptive view of Ben Avon above its lower neighbours to the north of Braemar.

Approaching from the Drumochter Pass and heading towards Dalwhinnie and on towards Newtonmore, the view is dominated by the Monadliath – the 'grey mountains' lying to the north of the Spey. Not until you are near Newtonmore and the road swings to the north-east do you first glimpse the western ramparts of the Cairngorms – whose old name was the Monad Ruadh or 'red mountains' – the great ridge which climbs out of the Rothiemurchus Forest to Creag Dhubh and then, higher still, to the summits of the Sgorans and on to the Carn Ban Mor. Even into June, the crest of this ridge is often patterned with snow, with long ribbons remaining in the gullies below the Sgorans and at the top of the Allt Fearniasan near the Carn Ban Mor. The eye is drawn to the deep recess of Coire Garblach. From the summits the view descends to the band of remnant native pinewood on the steep slopes of Creag Mhigeachaidh, then to the dark regular conifer stands in the Inshriach Forest, and further to the foreground of wind rippled

Looking to the northern ridges of the Cairngorms across Abernethy Forest and the scattered native pines of the Nethy moorlands. First are Craig nan Gall and the Pass of Ryvoan, followed by the top of Lurchers Gulley, with the Braeriach plateau on the far side of Lairig Ghru.

sedges in the Spey Marches which stretch down to Loch Insh.

The approaches which relate to the geography of roads will probably remain favoured by most visitors. However there are alternatives which bring special rewards. For example, to approach the Cairngorms on foot from the south-west by walking through Glen Tilt, enables one to experience this mountain region in an almost unique way when, towards the end of a long day's walk, the mountains gradually reveal themselves as you round the shoulder at the watershed between the Tilt and the Dee and gradually descend towards the ruins of Bynack Lodge. Or, one can walk south from Nethybridge, following the Nethy River through the great pine forest of Abernethy and up on to the high moorlands. This leads to Ryvoan and the deep long pass of the Lairig an Laoigh which separates the central and eastern Cairngorm blocks. Neither of these two approaches is for the impatient and may require a night to be spent out in the hills if the approach is to be followed by a penetration of the central massif.

III

In wandering the valleys we will have noticed the abundance of trees, not just the extensive plantations but the rich variety at the roadside – the birch, oak, bird cherry, pine and alder. We will also have glimpsed the remnants of more natural woodlands which we must now enter, for these natural woodlands of the Cairngorms have a special character and a relation to the area as a whole which is not to be found elsewhere.

We know from remains in the peat, and from the pollen record, that the Cairngorms were clothed in forest up to about 2000 feet for most of the last five thousand years. We don't know the detailed character of this primeval forest, but for most of this time, it was dominated by Scots pine and birch, though oak and alder may have been common in the valleys. The remains of this original forest cover are represented by the pine and birch woods of Speyside and Deeside which include some of the largest fragments of semi-natural woodland left in Britain.

The term semi-natural is frequently used when speaking of the vegetation, or of the animal and plant communities, of the wilder parts of Britain – in recognition of the fact that almost all of it has been modified to some degree by man's activities. This is particularly the case with woodlands. The term does introduce a distinction which is at least questionable because it implies that man's influence is not part of nature, whereas it could be argued that the modifications brought about by man's influence are indeed part of the natural process of the evolution of the earth's surface. Nevertheless, it is meaningful to distinguish areas which have a cover of largely native plants and animals from those where these have been substantially replaced by cultivated crops and domesticated animals.

In most parts of the world the lower slopes of mountains are forest covered and where this is not the case, as in much of Britain including Scotland, it is often because the forests have been destroyed through man's intervention, direct or indirect, mainly in historic, though sometimes extending back into pre-historic times.

The place names of the Cairngorms indicate a once much more extensive forest cover. Thus Kingussie comes from the Gaelic 'Cinn a Ghuithsaich', which means the head of the pinewood,

Old bushy topped native pine in the Rothiemurchus Forest.

though the town is now far up valley from the present main fragments of the pine. Perhaps, in earlier times the extensive pinewood gave way at Kingussie to the more open birchwoods of the upper part of the Spey Valley.

So part of the mountain experience is to be able to walk through woodlands before reaching the open slopes during the ascent, or when descending, to experience again the more sheltered conditions, and the evocative scent of resin from the pines, after having been exposed to the elements on the heights. This can still be part of the Cairngorm experience, though it is becoming rare elsewhere in Britain where the plantation forests generally provide a much less rewarding alternative – though the managed mountain forests in places like France, Germany or Switzerland show that this need not always remain the case. So we choose a route which will lead us through the woods and we enter into them. And the fact that we enter into them is meaningful. Our relation to them is not superficial, we enter into the woods and they enclose us. This fact is potent in human history and psychology, for humanity has an ambivalent relation to the forests which have, at different places and at different times, been regarded as either a threat or a refuge. The facts seem to suggest that few peoples have chosen to live in forests without creating a clearing, an open space, to live in. But of course one can choose to regard forest clearings as also being part of the forest.

We walk into the Rothiemurchus pinewoods, one of the largest remnants of the old pine forest in Speyside, and the question arises – where did we enter the wood? Where does the open ground finish and the woodland begin? Was it when we drove past the Coylumbridge Hotel and started noticing the scattered old pines and juniper? Or was it when we left the road and walked among the

The Rothiemurchus-Inshriach forest on the northern slopes of the Cairngorms by Loch Gahmna. Native pine and birch are slowly recolonising the old fellings on the terraces formed by glacial deposits.

close grown young trees? Already, in the sub-urban fringe, there was a scattering of old pinetrees, juniper bushes and many of the characteristic plants of the woodland floor. Natural woodlands don't usually have sharp edges like a plantation so it is not often easy to decide where they stop and the moorland begins and thus to say accurately how extensive the woodland is.

We notice the great size of many of the trees – most of them look old and tree ring studies have confirmed that the greater the girth the older the tree – though this doesn't hold when comparing trees from the bottom of the wood with those at the top. Many of the trees are between 150 and 200 years old. There are some dense stands of young trees near the road but not many of intermediate age. The old trees have broad crowns and some are gnarled and contorted. It seems that for most of the life span of the old trees that we see there hasn't been much regeneration, probably due to deer grazing – but that there has been quite a lot in some places during the last 20 to 25 years, not only of pine but also of juniper and some birch, where human disturbance has reduced the deer pressure – is this to be regarded as a 'natural' event or not? The wood is irregular, there are some large areas where the stumps of war-time felling are still discernible and where there is no regeneration. Elsewhere there are few signs of direct human intervention though it is a moot point to what extent the overwhelming dominance of the pine is an entirely natural feature. It has been suggested that it might be partly due to past extraction of less valuable timber species and differential removal by grazing, so that a lowered grazing pressure would enable a wider range of trees such as birch, bird cherry and rowan to co-exist with the pine in a more naturally diverse wood.

The diversity in the pinewoods is not just in the way that the

Cairngorm seen from Loch a Chnuic in the Abernethy Forest.

trees are disposed in the woods. Studies on the chemistry of the pine needles has shown that there are regional differences between the pines, so that the trees in the eastern pinewoods of the Cairngorms are genetically distinct from those in the Wester Ross pinewoods and also from those in the south-west Scotland remnants. Within individual woods there is also much more diversity among the pines than in any pine plantation. Some of the differences in growth form probably relate to the early history of the individual tree – whether it was browsed by deer or not – but other variables, including both tree form and the character and colour of the wood, seem to be genetic in origin. One common growth variant is spiral grain, remarkably demonstrated in a tree in Glen Derry struck by lightning some years ago, where the strike appeared to follow the water carrying vessels in the wood and cut a deep spiral groove from top to bottom of the tree trunk.

A feature of the pinewoods in central Glen Quoich, which I first noted in 1976, is the number of great old trees lying dead, all with the same orientation. It seems likely that these are the same ones which were observed by Seton Gordon in 1925. He reported that they had been blown down by a great northerly gale in 1893, but local tradition has it that some were uprooted by the storm which destroyed the Tay Bridge on 28th December 1879. They have been preserved by being supported clear of the ground by their side branches and have consequently been much slower to rot. Considerations of regeneration and diversity are particularly urgent in the old pinewood fragments on the southern slopes of the Cairngorms, such as those of Glen Derry and Glen Quoich where the problem was recognised long ago by Seton Gordon. The deer pressure is such that virtually no tree seedlings of any species survive above heather height outside fenced enclosures. So while

Facing
Magnificent stands of Old Scots pine in the native woodland of Glen Quoich, but with no natural regeneration due to heavy grazing by deer.

Following pages
Native pines and birch on the lower slopes of Creag Folais and Creag Mhigeachaidh.

these old woods continue to be an asset of great national interest and beauty, and support birds such as the crested tit, Scottish crossbill and capercailzie, together with insects and plants which are peculiar to the pinewood community, they are also impoverished because natural regeneration is, in most areas, inadequate to provide for continued succession – and the diversity of the tree species present is unnaturally restricted, mainly through the impact of centuries of grazing pressure.

Most of the woods now standing represent successful natural regeneration about 200 years ago when the glens were more highly populated and when the deer were fewer and had a much wider range of woodland for winter shelter. One of the effects of the new afforestation over the past fifty years has been to exclude the increasing numbers of deer from the traditional overwintering areas and concentrate them on the localities containing the old unfenced native pinewood relicts, where even now many would die from starvation if they were not artificially fed in late winter and early spring.

This is not to say that red deer are not a natural component of the native pinewoods – but the number now grazing in several of the Cairngorm pinewoods greatly exceed the numbers that would allow any natural regeneration to take place. This imbalance between deer numbers and the ecological health of the deer range has been the subject of much study but cannot be easily resolved while the land use of the area is dominated by the present tradition of estate management for red deer. However there is an immediate need to exclude deer from significant areas within and adjacent to the old pinewood remnants, particularly those on the southern slopes of the Cairngorms, to enable a new generation of trees to become naturally established while the old trees remain viable.

IV

A diversity of views have been expressed over the last fifty years on the best way of ensuring the continuity of the native pinewoods. These arguments are both interesting and important because they epitomise the main themes and approaches to nature conservation philosophy and because the remnant pinewoods are a very scarce resource which was once much more widespread and formed one of the main habitats within which important elements of the Scottish flora and fauna developed. Although about 35 authenticated remaining fragments of the old Caledonian pine forest within the Scottish Highlands were identified by Steven and Carlisle in their classic book based on field work carried out in the 1950s, a very high percentage of the total area of remaining native pinewood is found within the Deeside and Speyside pinewoods of the Cairngorm area.

The main concerns are that there is insufficient regeneration within the existing remnant pinewoods to ensure their perpetuation, that many of the remnant areas are too small, and that efforts should be made to reconstitute this important wildlife habitat over more of its natural range in the Scottish Highlands.

There is general agreement in principle that natural regeneration is inadequate to sustain many of the woods but diverse opinions on the best solution to this particular problem. There have been arguments between those who consider that the over-riding factor preventing natural regeneration is grazing, mainly by red deer, and others who, while admitting the importance of grazing, argue

Within the forest of Abernethy.

that the ground has often become unsuitable for regeneration even in the absence of grazing. The former, generally the wildlife conservationists and naturalists, argue for extensive use of fencing to exclude deer from regeneration areas together with substantial reduction in deer numbers. The latter, generally foresters and landowners, argue for ground treatment and planting with pine of local provenance to replenish the woods. The two sides in the argument are not completely opposed as very few would argue against the desirability of promoting natural regeneration and reducing deer numbers in some localities and, similarly, most would admit some scope for ground preparation and planting. There are already examples of successful and generally accepted schemes adopting both approaches in the Highlands, some on National Nature Reserves.

Why then do the nature conservationists favour natural regeneration through deer exclusion and reduction of deer numbers and what is their case against widespread ground preparation and planting?

The conservationists might answer these questions along the following lines:

'We have no shortage in Britain of environments which have been substantially formed by man's intervention – all our urban, industrial, agricultural land, plantation forests and grouse moors are examples of this. However, we are very short of land where the various wildlife components, the diverse native species of plants and animals, are free to react together and establish and maintain themselves over long periods of time in a dynamic relationship. Where these areas do exist they are often among the most beautiful and interesting parts of our natural heritage, largely as a result of this freedom to develop with the minimum of human interference,

The valley of the Dee at Mar Lodge. A fringe of pine over the old fellings above the lodge, the scattered native pine remnants in Lower Glen Lui beyond, and heather moorland rising to the Sgor Mor – Sgor Dubh ridge.

in complex response to the forces of natural selection. If we start to manipulate these areas to any great extent then we shall impose upon them man centred ideas of what they should be – which are likely to reflect the fashion of the day rather than any fundamental understanding of the ecological complexities of the natural situation. The areas will become characteristic of a particular management fashion rather than reflecting the working out of the ecological possibilities closely attuned to environmental conditions. Natural regeneration on the other hand will tend to reflect this relation, which, although it may proceed according to some generally understood ecological principles will, in detail, be unforeseeable, in response to complex interactions that cannot be forecast. It will probably involve species other than pine which will react with the existing vegetation in a way that cannot be prejudged. If we move towards ground preparation and planting, we will impose man centred concepts and reduce the natural diversity in areas which have not suffered this before. Nevertheless there are areas within the range of natural pine, though not within the existing pinewoods, where it would be worthwhile to use techniques such as ground preparation and planting of appropriate native pine stock, to try to reconstruct pinewoods having many of the characteristics of the native type and providing habitats for many of the characteristic pinewood species. You make the mistake of confusing the wood with the trees while we consider the wood to be the whole community of different tree and shrub species and the other animals and plants associated with them.'

The conservation argument has been strengthened by evidence which has accumulated to show that natural regeneration will take place in, and adjacent to, most pinewoods if grazing is substantially reduced even within the most apparently unfavourable ground

Coire Odhar, the head of Glen Einich with its stream cascading a thousand feet from the high plateau of the Moine Mhor.

conditions – though it may take much longer than if the ground were artificially disturbed and will not produce the regularity of trees preferred for commercial timber production. However the latter should not be of primary consideration in the rare pinewood remnants, though it could be an aim in the reconstituted pinewoods of native type elsewhere.

In the long term, the Cairngorm landscape and wildlife heritage will be enriched if the native woodlands are enabled to recolonise some of their former range on the lower slopes so that the natural sequence of native forest, moorland, plateau and summit is once more widely established, instead of being confined to the present small sectors on the periphery of the range. One of the problems is that we have become either accustomed to the treeless character of the approaches to the hills or depressed by the generally very negative experience provided by the new monoculture plantations on their lower slopes. This loss of sensitivity was commented upon over two thousand years ago by the Chinese sage Meng Tsu in one of the earliest statements on the ecological effects of grazing that I know of:

There was once a fine forest on the Ox mountain
Near the capital of a populous country
The men came out with axes and cut down the trees.
Was it still a fine forest?
Yet, resting in the alternation of days and nights
Moistened by dew
The stumps sprouted, the trees began to grow again.
Then out came goats and cattle to browse on the young shoots
The Ox mountain was stripped utterly bare
And people, seeing it stripped utterly bare
Think the Ox mountain never had any woods on it at all.

The treeless moors of Central Glen Avon near Linn of Avon – 'and people, seeing it stripped utterly bare . . . think it never had any woods on it at all.'

V

The perception of mountains involves the experience of transitions and one of the most obvious is that of the treeline, the place where the forest gives way to open moorland. Because the Cairngorm forests occupy only part of their potential range, this transition is only experienced on a few routes to the hill – and in even fewer does the tree line assume a more or less natural character.

Through encountering tree remains in the peat, miles from the nearest existing woodlands, most Cairngorm walkers realise that in the past the woodlands were much more extensive and extended further up the hill than at present. On most of the Cairngorm slopes where trees occur, they seldom go above about 1600 ft and in most of these cases we can hardly talk about a 'tree line' but rather of the level to which the old forests have died back, largely due to grazing and burning. A natural treeline, whether advancing or retreating, has a greater diversity of tree form and types of tree. It is not simply the place where the trees stop and has practically nothing in common with the upper boundary of a plantation, other than that the trees tend to be rather smaller for their age than those lower down.

Where the slopes are steep the treeline can be quite an abrupt feature, where they are gentle it is more of a broad zone – but still recognisable from a distance as a boundary, though when standing within it this aspect may not be so readily appreciated. All mountain treelines are more abrupt than the great change found in northern latitudes from forest to tundra. Treelines are one of the

Facing

The Rothiemurchus treeline at the north end of the Lairig Ghru between Castle Hill and Carn Elrig – 'and we step beyond the treeline and feel we are in a different world.'

Following pages

Rothiemurchus Forest from Ord Ban by Loch an Eilein, where trees reach 2000 ft at the treeline on the crest of Cadha Mor. The Cairngorm – Ben Macdhui plateau merges with that of Braeriach in the distance.

great transitions between major habitat forms of the natural world and they are always changing, though the life span of man may not be long enough to directly experience this dynamic. Trees and shrubs are continually seeding into the moorland beyond the treeline. Most of the seedlings perish but some establish themselves to grow to heather height where they may linger for many years pruned down by grazing or wind action, yet ready for an opportunity to continue their growth and advance the treeline if grazing declines or the climate improves. And, of course, the tree-line may retreat, as it has done for most of the past 200 years or longer in the Cairngorms, where trees dying at the margins have not been replaced by regeneration. Something approaching a natural treeline can be found on the northern slopes of the Cairngorms on the upper margins of the Rothiemurchus forest. The best known example is on the western flanks of Creag Fhiaclach where the forest reaches a height of 2100 feet. As one approaches the limits of the forest the trees decrease in stature till they are little more than the height of a man. Though dwarfed by the wind, they are still capable of surviving for hundreds of years and setting seed into the moorland above, where seedlings may commonly be found in the heather several hundred feet beyond the last grown tree. Birch and juniper accompany the pine as they would be expected to at a natural treeline.

So we step beyond the treeline and feel we are in a different world, and in a sense we are because in the primeval landscape, where the mountain forests were simply the upper extension of forests which covered the whole land, this would have been a breathtaking transition. Possibly even now, subconscious recognition of this accounts for why many people do not feel they are really on the mountain before they have left the treeline behind and have the

A distant view of Meall an
Lundain and Glen Quoich,
glimpsed from the Morrone
Birkwood National Nature Reserve
near Braemar.

extensive mountain vistas before them. Perhaps to reside within a
forest involves a limitation of vision to what immediately surrounds
us so that while we learn to appreciate the detail of our
surroundings, we tend to lose sight of the wider horizons of being.
Much early human activity in mountain areas took place close to,
but just above, the treeline.

Having made this transition I have sometimes recognised in
myself a tendency for the mind to focus too immediately on the
higher reaches of the mountain, anticipating the experience of the
plateau and peaks, and in so doing, traversing the lower unwooded
slopes, which lack the particular power of the forest to absorb us, in
a way which is unreceptive to their qualities. Taken to extremes
this attitude may lead to everything on the approaches becoming a
tiresome preliminary, even an irrelevance, to the object of a
particular summit or climb. Perhaps this reflects an inbuilt tendency
to overlook the commonplace, because the lower unwooded slopes
of the Cairngorms share much of their character with other
extensive Grampian moorlands, but it can lead to an
impoverishment of our experience.

> Only as a patch of hillside may be a cliché corner
> To a fool who cries "Nothing but heather!" where in
> September another
> Sitting there and resting and gazing round
> Sees not only heather but blaeberries
> With bright green leaves and leaves already turned scarlet.
> Hiding ripe blue berries; and among the sage-green leaves
> Of the bog-myrtle the golden flowers of the tormentil shining ...

> (MacDiarmid, from 'Scotland small ?', 1943)

However in the midge season there is every incentive to pass rapidly through these lower regions.

There is a general agreement among ecologists that the Cairngorm slopes below about 2000 feet belong to the 'forest zone' whether they actually carry forest or not. This is an insightful rather than a purely academic distinction. The removal of trees has resulted in a community of organisms, both plants and animals, which in some ways is more uniform, some might even say monotonous, than the original forest cover or the communities found at higher levels. But at the same time it is more dynamic, having lost the stability conferred by the presence of such long lived beings as the pine trees, yet lacking the restraints placed on communities at the higher levels by the severity of climate. These lower unwooded slopes are the areas containing the greatest intrinsic potential for change.

Because of its extensiveness, much of our time is spent within the limits of the forest zone and it is worth spending a little time considering its character and dynamic qualities.

When the trees disappeared, these forest zone areas became dominated by dwarf shrubs, predominantly by heather, and heather is a very interesting plant – its ecology in the Cairngorms could, by itself, form the subject of an absorbing book. It is present from the bottom to near the very top of the hills but its character and role in the vegetation varies greatly between the two. Heather occurs throughout the native pinewoods as a part of the ground vegetation but doesn't seem to be fully 'at home' there – where the tree canopy becomes denser, the heather becomes sparser and blaeberry and cowberry take over dominance. Neither does it thrive where birch becomes a common component of the forest tree cover. So, within the forest zone, it is likely that heather originally flourished

Ben Avon with its rocky summit tors and the River Avon.

only within the open spaces of the pine forest, as for example, at the margins of forest bogs. In some respects, the heather dominated moors represent a downward extension of a 'mountain' or 'alpine' zone community, made possible by the removal of the trees. This has had a fundamental influence on the distribution of animals dependent on heather, which must have been largely confined to the heather areas above the forest zone but which can now range much more widely. Notable are the grouse and associated predators like the Golden Eagle, which are as a result, far more abundant now than they could ever have been when their range was more restricted.

VI

The main distinction within the forest zone moorlands, and one that is particularly evident to the off-track walker, is the difference between the wet and the dry. Most of the Cairngorm granite area is relatively well drained but, particularly on the lower gentle slopes and in the valleys where drainage is impeded, peat has accumulated over thousands of years to form the deep peat valley bogs and shallower peat over gentle slopes known to the ecologist as 'blanket bogs'. Bogs are not so extensive in the Cairngorms as in the mountain areas of the North and West Highlands where there is higher rainfall, and heather tends to remain a common constituent of the Cairngorm bog vegetation. However, when seen from a distance, the wet heathery areas on the blanket bogs have a

Peatland pools below the Northern Corries of Cairngorm, looking towards the symmetrical cone of Airgiod-meall with Loch Dubh a Chadha at its base and the Monadliath mountains across the Spey beyond.

different shade due to the abundance of deer sedge. The deeper valley peat surfaces are generally recognisable from a distance by their characteristic dark brown edged surface drainage pattern, as seen on the floor of Glen Einich. In the upper part of the forest zone, above 1500 feet, peaty moorland often contains an abundance of the cloudberry, though this extends up into the higher mountain zone peatlands.

Wet moorlands provoke an awareness of their intricate mosaic because of the need to become adept at avoiding the wetter bog-moss dominated areas and searching out footfalls on the drier heather knolls or deer sedge clumps. However peatland is vulnerable to trampling and is best avoided for conservation reasons as well as for ease of passage.

Peat-forming tendencies have varied over the ages. Studies of the peat structure and pollen content have shown that there was a period of climatic deterioration 2-3,000 years ago, round about the transition from the Bronze Age to the Iron Age, when peat growth was much accelerated and the treeline descended. The further decline of the forest under human influence may also have helped to maintain peat growth because, in drier periods, trees can invade peat areas and accelerate their drying out.

The other great variation in the Cairngorm heather moors is that caused by fire. In the grouse moors on the periphery of the Cairngorms, and eastwards into Aberdeenshire, the patchwork caused by the annual sequence of burns is the most dominant feature in the landscape – though this is not a prominent feature of the main central Cairngorm area where burning has generally been related to sheep rather than grouse management. With the reduction of the forest and the extension of the heather moors within the forest zone, the landscape must generally have become much more

The spectacular glacial trough of Glen Einich from the air with Loch Mhic Ghille Coille in the foreground and Loch Einich in the shadow beyond. On the right, the ramparts of the Sgorans, and above the head of the glen, the remote plateau of the Moine Mhor. In the distance, the peaks of Atholl.

inflammable because although there is evidence to show that natural fires have always been a feature of coniferous forests, and they occur there at relatively infrequent intervals, the heaths above the forest zone are generally much less inflammable than those lower down.

The history of grouse moors has shown that heather can continue to flourish, and to provide young shoots for maintaining the artificially high populations of grouse, which are the aim of grouse moor management, for a very long time if subject to periodic burning of small patches at a 12 to 15 year interval. However if it is burned more frequently, and particularly if heavy grazing by sheep accompanies the burning, then the heather moorland is gradually converted into grass or sedge dominated plant communities. This has happened extensively in the Western Highlands, in the Southern Uplands and in the mountain areas of England and Wales where the disappearance of heather has reached alarming proportions. Generally, this decline of heather has not taken place extensively in the Cairngorms because the soils are too deficient in nutrients to sustain the density of grazing animals which would convert the heather moorland into grass or sedge vegetation. In fact grassland is quite a rare vegetation type within the Cairngorm forest zone, occurring mainly on valley floors subject to occasional flooding or on low level outcrops of lime rich schists on the periphery of the range.

Three other dwarf shrubs of the same plant family, blaeberry, cowberry and bearberry, have an interesting relationship with heather in the forest zone. With increasing shade under the pines, blaeberry and cowberry become dominant while heather becomes scarce. In open moorlands cowberry and bearberry frequently form a subsidiary layer to the heather. Where the ground has been

Facing
Beinn a Bhuird and the middle altitude grouse moors above Glen Quioch, showing heather burn patches.

Following pages
The River Eidart, draining south from the high plateau of the Moine Mhor. Serried ridges of relict glacial deposits on right.

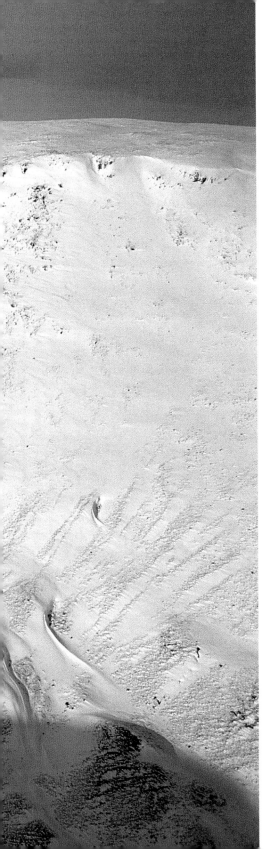

disturbed, as along the side of a recently constructed road, bearberry may become dominant, and the lighter green of areas burned one or two years ago is due to the dominance of blaeberry in the early succession back to heather cover.

Blaeberry dominated patches in the lower moorlands, generally in crescent shaped hollows or shallow gullies, are often indicative of long-lying snow beds as blaeberry can tolerate this much more readily than heather. This is the first example of the cause of a pattern in the vegetation which becomes much more significant at higher altitudes above the forest zone.

The absence of trees in the forest zone makes it easier to see some of the remarkable landforms due to past glaciation which are so characteristic of the Cairngorm area. Many of these occur throughout Speyside and Deeside, which were main channels of ice flow during the Ice-Age, and are very evident on aerial photographs of the area but not so easily observed when within the level wooded glens. Within the forest zone these often take the form of terraces along the side of glens and elongated mounds, both of which were formed of water layered sands and gravels under great ice sheets which largely submerged the Cairngorms during the Ice Age, as in the case of the great ridge which almost cuts off the bottom of the Northern Corries save for the passage of the Allt Mor, or at the sides of valley glaciers like the terraces near the bottom of Glen Einich. Elsewhere they occur as clusters of hillocks on the gentle lower slopes of glens, such as appear in upper Glen Derry and Glen Geusachan and are sometimes referred to as 'hummocky moraines', though some of these may have been formed by water deposition under a stagnant ice sheet rather than on top of an active glacier like true moraines.

VII

The transition between the moorlands of the forest zone and the higher moorlands is less obvious than a treeline and generally takes place between about 2000 and 3000 feet, depending on aspect and exposure. The character of the landscape also changes at this altitude, the relatively uniform lower slopes giving way to a landscape in which corries, cliffs and screes create a much more complex terrain.

Ecologists have recognised several zones above the treeline. A heather dominated zone up to about 3000 feet, a zone dominated by crowberry and blaeberry between about 3000 feet and 3500 feet and a zone comprising the high plateau and summits over 3200 feet characterised by the three pointed rush. Whilst this is a useful generalisation, it obscures the complex and fascinating relationships between the plant communities, the landforms, climate and mountain processes at the higher levels.

If you walk south along the great ridge that rises out of the Rothiemurchus forest, either from the near natural treeline of Creag Fhiaclach or the neighbouring spur of Cadha Mor and then climb to the Sgorans, you pass through sequences of most of these zones except that of the highest plateau and summit.

On leaving the trees at about 2100 feet the heather is at first deep with a few stunted pines, probably 20 to 30 years old, no higher than the heather. Dwarf juniper are to be found creeping among bouldery patches. In the hills of Norway this would be the zone where one would expect to find a dense scrub of dwarf willow,

Coire Garblach and the plateau of the Moine Mhor above Glen Feshie. The scar defacing the spur to the right of the corrie is a bulldozed stalking track. This corrie is cut mainly into schists and is of very different character from the majority of the Cairngorm Corries in the granite.

dwarf birch and juniper, but here in the Cairngorms there are only traces to suggest that such a community may once have been widespread. Approaching the crest of the ridge the heather quickly decreases in stature and forms a mat with bell heather and deer sedge.

Nearing the crest of the ridge, the first of the boulder edged lobes which garland the upper slopes of much of the Cairngorms appear – indications of mountain processes of severer climates in the past which were capable of moving great masses of surface material slowly down the slopes. Here the surfaces of the lobes are well vegetated and the boulders forming the fronts are bedded in the turf and moss and lichen covered. This, the first of a series, loops away to join with others in a line along the contour on the flanks of the ridge.

When even the slightest depression gives shelter, the heather and bell heather grow more luxuriantly and flower more abundantly, forming a colourful patch among the more subdued shades of the surrounding vegetation mat, which here is made up of the tightly interlacing shoots of dwarf heather, bearberry, crowberry and lichens. In more sheltered areas, patches of peat support denser vegetation with an abundance of cloudberry. Signs of vegetation instability appear in the form of small circular lenses of bare soil and stones – 'stony earth circles' where the exposed surface still bears the traces of the spring's frost heaving.

Higher up the ridge, at over 2500 feet, occur the first of the frost formed terraces, running across the contour on the crest of the ridge so one steps directly over the heather clad risers on to the bare gravelly treads. Here the processes of frost, rain and wind are still active and the granite gravel spills over the edge of the risers, feeding the gradual motion of the steps downslope. Near the first

Derry Cairngorm and the cliffs of Coire Sputan Dearg on Ben Macdhui.

summit, Creag Dhubh at 2700 feet, mountain azaleas join the plants in the tightly woven mat of vegetation.

Descending a little to the saddle before the final climb to Sgoran Dubh Mor – a marvellous carpet of heather, crowberry, blaeberry and lichens ornamented by occasional heather flowers and the black crowberries.

Climbing to over 3000 feet – the surface of garland lobes covered by a beautifully rippled mat of woolly hair moss, with Bigelows sedge and crowberry. In the sheltered embayments between the lobes, where snow is trapped in winter, a quite different plant community grows, rich in dwarf blaeberry and the bog blaeberry.

VIII

The Cairngorm plateau in winter. The summit of Cairngorm is in the foreground, with the Braeriach plateau in the middle distance, and on the horizon, the Drummochter and Ben Alder peaks.

These Cairngorm slopes and the plateaux and summits above, their animals, plants, geology and landforms, have been the subject of much study for over two centuries. The question occurs – does acquaintance with this vast store of accumulated knowledge add to our appreciation and enjoyment of the hills? Sometimes knowledge, in terms of sheer information or ideas can seem an impediment to our experience, so that we wander theory ridden in the hills as if with tinted spectacles, and don't actually see anything uncoloured by our own preconceptions, which even if they give us the comfort of familiarity, can render us insensitive to new impressions. The scientist may be particularly vulnerable to this tendency which is felt by some to manifest in a deadening effect, evident in much scientific literature, stemming from the scientific tradition of reductionism and objectivity. However perhaps this is, in part, simply a symptom of specialisation which is no different in kind from the apparently limited appreciation of the hills which can sometimes be met in skiers and rock climbers – at least in the way they express themselves about their experiences. But although the appreciation of the mountains which emerges from science contains this specialised aspect of knowledge, the wish to understand may be more fundamental and lead to a deep sympathy with the subjects of study – a 'feeling for the organism' in the words of the American scientist Barbara McClintock. One has to admit the possibility that to intimately know the life of one ptarmigan, from its birth to its death on the Ben Macdhui plateau, may lead to a greater understanding of the Cairngorms than a lifetime of walking from end to end. Ultimately, though, it becomes invidious to attempt to compare and evaluate the personal experience of mountains, which can be different for each person on each occasion and yet even then represent only an infinitesimally small part of the possible. But cultivating a 'feeling for the organism' whether midge, mouse or mountain, is perhaps the key to the unselfish enjoyment of the hills.

Walking up from open moorland into a corrie, the increasing sense of enclosure, of entering a special place, and corries have long been recognised as being special places, there are over forty of them in the Cairngorms and they all have names. Coire an t-Sneachda – Corrie of the snow, Coire an Lochain Uaine – Corrie of the Green Lochan, Coire Etchachan – Corrie of great space.

Monad Ruadh – the 'Red Mountains'. The Northern Corries in summer, looking towards Cairngorm, with Lurcher's Gully in the foreground.

Lying on one's back on a great corrie boulder in summer sunshine, thinking of glaciers. Blue sky above, quietness but not silence, lapping of waters from the lochan, a rattle of stones from the great cliffs of the headwall rising behind. All around a chaos of boulders – no, not a chaos, they are all in their place and far from random. Moraines beyond the lochan closing out the world beyond. Corrie, cwm – the hollow that is enclosed, but in French 'cirque', that which encloses. Two perspectives at this moment – wherein does the quality of the corrie lie, in the emptiness or in the form?

Studies have shown that the Cairngorm corries fall into two groups – a group with floors at the 1900 ft-2300 ft level which are almost all facing east, opening into the north-south glens, and a more numerous group with floors about 2600 to 3100 ft, most of which are north facing. The predominantly north to east orientation stems from the pattern of major snow accumulation, the snow blown by the prevailing south-westerlies off the plateau, and trapped in hollows which, in times of severe climate, accumulated to form glaciers which scraped out the characteristic symmetry of the corrie form. It seems that all the main Cairngorm corries resulted from the action of corrie glaciers before the ice sheet covered all the mountains. Little trace remains of the vast quantity of rock that represents the hollow of the corries – it was all ground down and swept away by the ice movement of the subsequent overriding ice sheet.

In only eight of the corries are there moraines which indicate the presence of small corrie glaciers subsequent to the wasting of the ice sheet, but these have made only small changes to the original form of the corrie. Most of these corrie moraines were

Facing
Looking down Coire Garblach to Glen Feshie and the Spey Valley with the snow covered Monadliath, the 'Grey Mountains', in the distance.

Following pages
Coire an Lochan of the Northern Corries, with its sheltered tarn and summer snowbeds.

probably formed about 10,000 years ago, but a few look more recent and there is some evidence that these corries may have held large permanent snow beds, if not incipient glaciers, in the Middle Ages and up to the 18th Century – the period of the so called 'Little Ice-Age' when alpine glaciers were much larger than at present. Some early travellers in the Cairngorm area such as Taylor (1618) and Pennant (1771) commented on the permanent snow at high altitude.

IX

Turning to gaze up at the cliffs, foreshortened from here. There isn't a great botanical diversity finding refuge on these granite rocks compared with the fringes of the range where the schists predominate, as in Glen Feshie but, on the ledges inaccessible to grazing animals, the mountain vegetation grows more luxuriantly. High ledges provide a nesting refuge for eagle, peregrine and that most evocative dweller in high corries, the raven. Tracing routes up the rock face, climbing in the mind, feeling in imagination the sharp crystalled granite under the fingers.

There is a long tradition of climbing in these corries going back to the early years of the century so that present day climbing guidebooks show a complex network of possibilities, or for the most of us, impossibilities. Has the cliff changed because of this? To some extent yes. On more frequented routes all the vegetation has long since gone, leaving the 'clean' rock preferred by the climber, and the nailed boots of the early decades produced distinct abrasion that can still be recognised. But times and fashions change and the vegetation reinvades where man ceases to go.

Only the skiing corries have been permanently transformed so that never again in the life of living generations will their natural character be experienced. The bulldozed road scars and the clutter of ski lift and snowfencing are the price paid for the enjoyment of the skier during those few months when skiing is possible. There was skiing here before the constructions – but this was a kind that enjoyed what the mountain had to offer without demanding anything extra of it, and of course this type of skiing still goes on away from the honeypots of Coire Cas and Coire na Ciste.

Winter climbing. To enter the corrie in winter, stumbling through deep powder snow or treading the crisp frozen surface. A transformed world of white and ice blue-green and snow muffled silence. Weak winter sun glinting on the snow devils dancing on the corrie rim, the cliffs in shadow. Cramponning up hard packed snow and surmounting the cornice to emerge on to the arctic plateau.

The upper slopes of Coire Cas on Cairngorm. 'The bulldozed road scars and clutter of ski lift and snow fencing are the price paid for the enjoyment of the skier during those few months when skiing is possible.'

X

That the Cairngorm summits are frequently indistinguishable from the plateau might seem to some a failing. The sense of purpose and achievement embodied in the concept of a summit is absent, for while the plateau is indeed a place having a particular character which can be experienced, we cannot, as in corrie or on peak, easily say where we have been. The place is not so easily encompassed with words.

Like the sea or an island we encounter the plateau, but it does not so readily feature as an object of possession. The psychology of conquest is not pandered to, it is not found in Munro's tables. Lacking the corrie's walls, its boundaries are defined by an airy openness and one feels a greater continuity between plateau and sky than between plateau and the lower ground.

The word 'plateau', deriving from the French, conveys little of the character of the place except its relative flatness. The Norwegians have a word for it, sometimes translated as 'fell-field' but saying more in the original tongue – 'fjellvidde', a wide place, a place having breadth, in the mountains. There are other high and wide places in the world's mountains – Mlanje, the Andean 'altiplano', and Tibet sharing this isolation beneath the skies, and having 'majesty great enough to cast a spell on man's mind.'

In fair summer weather the steep approach slopes gradually lessen and we find ourselves walking with relative ease into the heart of the plateau, the outer world disappearing below its rim.

The winter plateau of the Moine Mhor. 'A severe place, not hostile, but not without danger.'

71

Vegetation is sparse, the ground surface largely bare, though not barren, being mainly of granite or granite gravel and life, for both animals and plants, is precarious. Special qualities are needed for survival in these conditions and few living things have it. Nevertheless the plateau is a refuge for those which do.

On the ground most exposed to the wind, rock and gravel predominate. The great boulders, which often cover the ground surface and provide shelter for the windpruned plants in their lee, seldom lie on bedrock, which is often separated from them by several feet of weathered granite 'soil'. On flat surfaces, as in the vicinity of the Ben Macdhui and Beinn a Bhuird summits, these boulders form great sunken interlocking circles or 'polygons' about 6ft across with smaller stones or gravel in their raised centres, the remnants of arctic or 'periglacial' processes which took place when the subsoil was permanently frozen. These metamorphose into stone stripes where the ground gently slopes. These and other patterns can sometimes be seen from the air, underlying vegetation.

In some exposed granite gravel areas, the vegetation of dwarf heather, crowberry, least willow, three flowered rush or dwarf azalea, forms waves or crescents which move across the ground surface under the influence of the wind at a rate estimated to be about $1/2$ to 1 cm per year. Occasional patches of moss campion in flower provide a splash of colour. In autumn the whole plateau is chestnut tinged by the turning leaves of the three-flowered rush.

Sheltered hollows in the plateau surface accumulate snow which may lie for many months and be dominated by light coloured mat grass when the snow finally disappears. Where the snow lasts even longer and the ground remains wet, carpets of brown moss occur speckled with occasional plants of the dwarf cudweed and Sibbaldia.

Beinn Bhreac, the 'speckled hill', the patterns painted by rain, snow, frost and wind.

The plant names reveal their mountain or arctic affinities – the lichen *Cetraria islandica*, the moss *Polytrichum norvegicum*, even the rigid sedge *Carex bigelowii*, named after the North American botanist Jacob Bigelow, from a specimen collected in the White Mountains of New Hampshire, for many arctic plants are circumpolar in their distribution. Many of the insects and spiders which live in the vegetation mat or under the stones – *Miscodera arctica, Otiorhynchus arcticus, Erigone tirolensis* – also have arctic and alpine affinities.

Indeed for many of the plants and animals of the plateau, their home is an arctic island and their nearest neighbours are on other mountain tops, the Faroes, Iceland and Spitzbergen. Sharing this type of circumpolar distribution is one of the most characteristic birds of the plateau, the ptarmigan, always present to intrigue by its indescribable call or to surprise by bursting forth from among the boulders in a flurry of grey and white. Its dress matches the changing season, though sometimes, like the mountain hare, it is deceived by an unseasonal lack of snow when its white plumage stands out sharply against the rocks or dark dwarf heather. Only in the heaviest snows does it desert the plateau to frequent the lower moors where heather becomes its main food instead of the favoured shoots and berries of crowberry or blaeberry.

The Braeriach plateau from the air. Garbh Choire on the left.

XI

These plateau communities are a strange mixture of toughness, resilience and fragility. The toughness reflects their close adaptation to their severe domain, the scouring winds, the frequent change between freeze, thaw and freeze – even in early summer the exposed soil is still bloated underfoot from the spring's frost-heave. Great sheets of vegetation are sometimes stripped off by the wind, later to slowly recolonise. Ptarmigan can adapt to some extent to the mere presence of people and maintain their numbers so long as they are not deprived of their food supplies, yet this close adaptation to natural severity is more usually paralleled by a sensitivity to disturbance to which there has not been, or perhaps cannot be, any adaptation. The sparse vegetation of the plateau can be badly damaged by trampling and the destructive effects of driving a vehicle once over the high altitude moss heaths can last for over twenty years. Litter and refuse attract scavengers which would not normally frequent the area but which, once attracted, can turn their attention to the eggs and young of rare plateau breeding birds.

Recollections of the plateau in winter – and winter can be experienced on the plateau any time between September and June. A severe place, not hostile, but not without danger. A place to be trodden with respect and care. I had tasted Cairngorm winter storms on my first visit when, not wanting to waste a day we had set out from Luibeg to walk to the Corrour bothy. Rain, turning to sleet blew horizontally and quickly penetrated the ex-army

Facing
The view south-west from Beinn Mheadhoin across the hidden Coire Etchachan. The slopes of Ben Macdhui on the right.

Following pages
The Devil's Point and Glen Geusachan.

windproofs and boots which were our best mountain wear. As we crossed the rise at the head of Glen Lui and turned into the Lairig Ghru a great blast from the north hit us and within minutes, as we staggered forward against the wind, our outer clothing froze into an armour. We could not help but voice our wonder, if it is like this here, what must it be like on the plateau?

We chose not to seek the answer to that question, indeed we would never have got near the plateau on that day but retreated to the pine-log fire at Luibeg. In the next two days we traversed Ben Macdhui and climbed Cairn Toul, learning about the texture of Cairngorm snow, the endless breaking crusts, the bottomless fresh powdered snow in the high glens and corries, the hard wind-brushed snow and ice of the spurs, ridges and plateau. The low winter sun glared from the ice and new snow, sparkled on the deep rime which encased every rock and crag and cast deep blue shadows into the glens and corries. All the streams were silenced, frozen hard or running deep beneath the snow.

Standing on the hard crystalline snow of Cairn Toul summit – snow covered peaks in sunshine to the south and east but, from the north an ominous bank of cloud moving south towards us, enveloping Ben Macdhui, then Braeriach and investing Cairn Toul with an unearthly glow. A quick glissade to the Corrour bothy, walking back to Luibeg through the sunset of orange clouds and turquoise sky.

Winter storm on the plateau, wind and white-out. Almost impossible to face the wind, face and eyes stung by flying snow and ice crystals, sometimes blown off feet, difficult to see – and nothing to see, snow surface merging into blown snow and cloud. Reading map and compass crouched behind boulder a major operation, no place for an error and no time for an accident. Best be somewhere else, and that soon.

XII

Omitting from the earlier quotations the second part of the Meng Tsu text and the first line of the MacDiarmid poem obscures the fact that both are parts of an extended metaphor. Metaphors which draw parallels between man's appreciation of his surroundings and his spiritual or moral condition.

Meng Tsu goes on to observe that:

Our mind too, stripped bare like the mountain
Still cannot be without some tendency to love
But just as men with axes, cutting down the trees
Every morning
Destroy the beauty of the forest
So we, by our daily actions, destroy our right mind.

Adding MacDiarmid's initial line:

Scotland small? Our multiform, our infinite Scotland *small*?

completes a metaphor which points to the absurdities stemming from stunted sensibility.

By cultivating an awareness and understanding of places having the natural quality of the Cairngorms, we come to realise that with all the joy that such an acquaintance can bring, there is truth in the saying that 'nowhere upon earth does the rose of happiness blossom without thorns'. We begin to see the

The Lairig Ghru from the air. The fluted slopes of Sron na Lairig on the right, below the summits of the Devil's Point, Cairn Toul and Braeriach.

transformation of Meng Tsu's metaphor into an equivalence. The damage we do to ourselves by moral failing and the damage we do to the environment by insensitive use become indistinguishable. We no longer damage ourselves *like* we damage the mountains, we damage ourselves *and* the mountains by our actions, indeed we may come to realise that there are no selves separate from the mountain.

We now know that the Cairngorms are particularly sensitive to acid rain effects, especially those associated with snow melt. The climatic warming associated with the 'greenhouse effect' will probably have far ranging though as yet imponderable influences on the Cairngorm plants and animals. We know that maintenance of artificially high deer populations will lead to continued deterioration of all the deer range, including the forest remnants. We know that the use of vehicles on the hill will damage the terrain, and impair the walkers' appreciation of it, just as the bulldozed tracks have devastated the old stalking paths and rights of way and diminished the enjoyment of thousands of visitors over the last twenty-five years. We cannot un-know this insight, gained by the patient dedicated work of many having a 'feeling for the organism' that is the Cairngorms, and understanding of this sort transforms the Meng Tsu parable into a contemporary moral dilemma. Can we continue to recognise the Cairngorms as one of the finest mountain areas in Europe yet persist with a culture which will continually diminish its quality – without at the same time bringing about our own moral and spiritual diminution, and an atrophy of the ability to appreciate what we are losing?

So in this small area of the planet's surface which we call the Cairngorms we have a microcosm of the world's conservation problems – and an opportunity to work towards their solution. But did I say small? Cairngorms *small*?

Beinn Bhrotain in winter sunshine and spindrift.

82

SELECTED BIBLIOGRAPHY

Burton, J H — *The Cairngorm Mountains* (Edinburgh, 1864). The first book devoted to a description of the Cairngorms.

Gordon, S — *The Cairngorm Hills of Scotland* (Cassell, 1925). A classic work on the area.

Grant, E — *Memoirs of a Highland Lady* (Murray, 1898).

Keller, E F — *A Feeling for the Organism – The Life and Work of Barbara Mclintock* (Freeman, 1983).

MacDiarmid, H — *Anthology: Poems in Scots and English* (Routledge & Kegan Paul, 1972).

MacGillivray, W — *The Natural History of Deeside and Braemar* (London, 1855). The first authoritative work on the natural history of the Cairngorms.

Meng Tsu (Mencius) — *The Ox Mountain Parable.* The version here is from Merton, T – *Mystics and Zen Masters* (Delta Press, 1967), who adapted it from Richards, I A – *Mencius on the Mind* (London, 1932). See also Lau, D C – *Mencius* (Penguin Classics, 1970).

Murray, W H — *Highland Landscape* (National Trust Scotland, 1962).

Naess, A — *The Metaphysics of the Treeline* (Appalachia 188, 1989). A paper by the philosopher of the 'deep ecology' movement, stimulated by discussions in the Cairngorm pinewoods. See also Naess – *Modesty and the Conquest of Mountains*, found in – *The Mountain Spirit* (Gollancz, 1980), edited by Tobias & Drasdo.

Nethersole Thompson, C & Watson, A — *The Cairngorms* (Melven Press, 1981). The standard work on the Cairngorms and a valuable source of references.

Shepherd, N — *The Living Mountain: A Celebration of the Cairngorm Mountains in Scotland* (Aberdeen University Press, 1977). An affectionate appreciation of the character of the hills.

Steven, H M & Carlisle, A — *The Native Pinewoods of Scotland* (Oliver & Boyd, 1959). Still the standard work on the Cairngorm native pinewoods.

Watson, A & Allen, E J P — *The Place Names of Upper Deeside* (Aberdeen University Press, 1984). A wonderful source of thoughtful information about Cairngorm places.